Delaney
Street
Press

Gwen

A Sister Is...

Always Loved Catherine

'2000

A Sister Is...

A Treasury of Inspirational Quotations for Sisters

Compiled and Edited by

Mary Carlisle Beasley

DELANEY STREET PRESS
Nashville, TN: (800) 256-8584

ISBN 1-58334-061-0

The ideas expressed in this book are not, in all cases, exact quotations, as some have been edited for clarity and brevity. In all cases, the author has attempted to maintain the speaker's original intent. In some cases, material for this book was obtained from secondary sources, primarily print media. While every effort was made to ensure the accuracy of these sources, the accuracy cannot be guaranteed. For additions, deletions, corrections or clarifications in future editions of this text, please write DELANEY STREET PRESS.

Printed in the United States of America
Cover Design by Bart Dawson
Typesetting & Page Layout by Sue Gerdes

1 2 3 4 5 6 7 8 9 10 • 00 01 02 03 04 05 06

ACKNOWLEDGMENTS

The author gratefully acknowledges the helpful support of Angela Beasley Freeman, Dick and Mary Freeman, Mary Susan Freeman, Jim Gallery, and the entire team of professionals at DELANEY STREET PRESS and WALNUT GROVE PRESS.

For Mary Susan and Carli

Table of Contents

There is no friend like a sister, in calm or stormy weather.

Christina Rossetti

1

A Sister Is...

If you are blessed with a loving sister, give thanks. She is, as you know, a unique and special person in your life. Your sister is, in all likelihood, a friend, a counselor, and a cheerleader. She picks you up when you fall, and you do the same for her. She links you to your past, and the two of you share memories that are yours and hers alone.

This little collection of quotations celebrates the joys of sisterhood. On the pages that follow, savvy sisters share their insights and observations about that unique woman who will forever be an integral part of your life: your sister.

My sister is laughter, even on the cloudy days of life.

Lillian Gish

A sister is
a bundle of
blessings bound
together
by laughter
and love.

Angela Beasley Freeman

A sister is a friend —
someone we grew up with,
fought with, and learned from.

Arlene F. Benedict

From the early years of life,
sisters' union is one of the most
emotionally charged of
all relationships.

Dale V. Atkins

A sister can be seen as
someone who is both ourselves
and very much not ourselves —
a special kind of double.

Toni Morrison

A woman's best support is a dear sister.

Helen Stewart

A loyal sister is worth a thousand friends.

Marian Eigerman

To know a sister is to know
a paradox.

Patricia Foster

Sisters are our peers, the voice
of our times.

Elizabeth Fishel

Sisterhood is
a lifelong conversation.

Karen Brown

My sister never judges me. She's my best friend and the only person I know I can tell anything to.

Lorna Luft

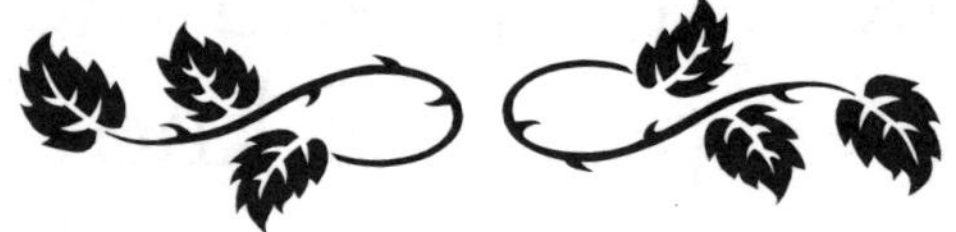

2

Love

The love between sisters is like no other. In youth, there may exist a fierce rivalry, but even then, the loving bond between young sisters continues to grow. And as the girls mature into women, a lifelong mutual appreciation begins to blossom.

Sisters share many things: memories, secrets, values, hopes, dreams, even clothes. But the greatest gift that two sisters can ever share is the gift of love. Wise sisters share that gift early and often.

A squabbling resulted from our sharing a bed for so many years...we usually made a "frontier" with sheet folds carefully separating our domains.

Alva Myrdal

When we were thirteen, our parents got us twin beds. Know what we did? We put a violin case in her bed, covered it up, and the two of us slept in mine. By fifteen, it got doggone crowded in there.

Abigail Van Buren
speaking of her sister Ann Landers

My sister and I slept in the same room in the same bed, and she always woke me up when she came in from a date. We'd lie there and whisper and giggle. I wanted to be just like her.

Minnie Pearl,
of her sister

Last night Margot and I were lying side by side in my bed. It was incredibly cramped, but that's what made it fun.

Anne Frank,
of her sister

While some sisters
are kindred spirits from
the very beginning,
I really began
to appreciate
my sister years later.

Alda Ellis

Is there any solace more comforting than the arms of a sister?

Alice Walker

Sisters shield us
from life's cruel circumstances.

Nancy Mitford

I feel about my sisters the way
a mother feels about her children...
like a mamma lion.

Barbara Mandrell

Whatever happens, I know my sisters
are there for me.

Patti Labelle

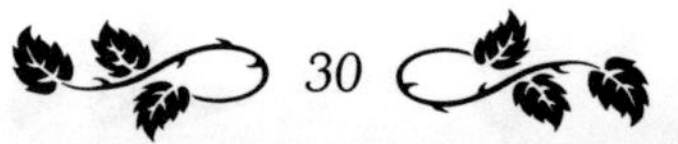

Some sisters never move beyond their childhood rivalry. Most, however, develop an affectionate attachment, a critical support system in their middle and later years.

Carol Saline

Sisters, while they are growing up, tend to be rivals...but as they grow older, sisters grow closer together.

Margaret Mead

You know as well as I do the value of sisters' affections for each other; there is nothing like it in the world.

Charlotte Brontë

I should love her even if she were not my sister; and even if she did not love me.

Elizabeth Barrett Browning

Sisters share a profound bond that seems to defy explanation.

Arlene F. Benedict

Good or bad, distant or apart, sisters are tuned into each other with an uncanniness that baffles outsiders.

Barbara Mathias

Meeting with a sister means coming face to face with images of your former self that still live in her mind's eye.

Brigid McConville

The human heart, at whatever age, opens to the heart that opens in return.

Maria Edgeworth

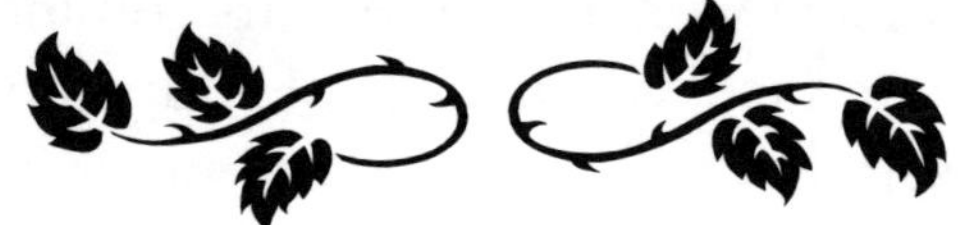

3

Sharing

Sisterhood is an exercise in sharing. During the early years, sisters share toys and clothes. In later years, they share hopes, dreams, feelings, and memories.

This world holds few blessings greater than that of a generous sister. The following quotations prove once and for all that it's a good thing for children to share their toys, but it's an even better thing for adults to share their time and their resources.

Sisters who have learned to share as children may go on sharing for the rest of their lives.

Brigid McConville

My sister was the first person I could tell the truth to.

Elizabeth Fishel

We shared parents.
Home. Pets.
Celebrations.
Catastrophes.
Secrets.
We are linked.

Pam Brown

One of the best things about being an adult is the realization that you can share with your sister and still have plenty left for yourself.

Betsy Cohen

Sharing is sometimes more demanding than giving.

Mary Catherine Bateson

Blessed are those who can give without remembering and take without forgetting.

Elizabeth Bibesco

Listening, not imitation,
is the sincerest form of flattery.

Dr. Joyce Brothers

You can't fake listening. It shows.

Raquel Welch

A sister is often the person who understands you best.

Janet Lanese

Trouble is part of your life. And, if you don't share it, you don't give the people who love you a chance to love you enough.

Dinah Shore

As we grow up, sisters serve as teachers, models, problem solvers, confidantes, catalysts, challengers, socializers, protectors, and caregivers.

Dale V. Atkins

Sisters fundamentally shape the kind of people we become.

Brigid McConville

Alone we can
do so little.
Together we can
do so much.

Helen Keller

Sisters are girlfriends, rivals,
listening posts, shopping buddies,
confidantes, and much, much more.

Carol Saline

My sister showed me
what was possible.

Lynn Redgrave

I would like more sisters, so that the talking out of one might not leave such stillness.

Emily Dickinson

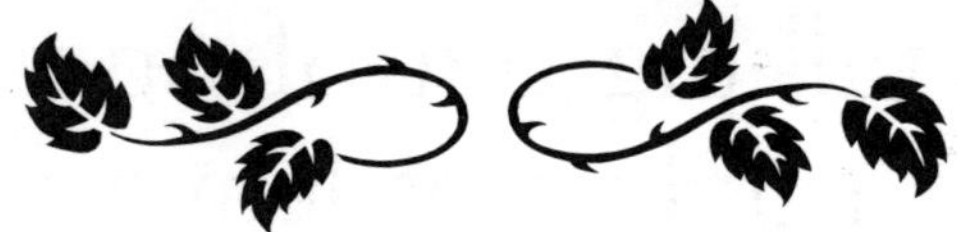

4

Family

Sisters, springing from the same family, share a rich heritage. Under the best of circumstances, family ties bind tightly yet comfortably throughout life. Loving sisters help tie that knot and keep it tight.

The quotations on the following pages remind us of a remarkable, lifelong, life-changing gift: a loving family.

I watched every move my older sister Dixie made. I couldn't wait to grow up so I could be like her.

Minnie Pearl

Families the world around are the place where people learn who they are and how to be that way.

Jean Illsley Clarke

Many years later, Madge had only to use the elder sister voice, and I would feel chills down my spine.

Agatha Christie

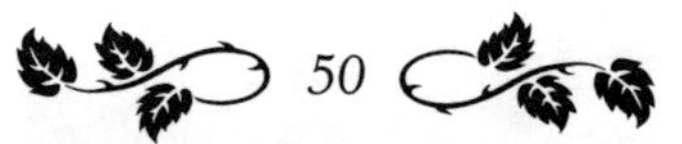

My sister taught me everything I needed to know, and she was only in the sixth grade at the time.

Linda Sunshine

Example is the school of humankind,
and they will learn at no other.

Edmund Burke

Nothing is so infectious as example.

La Rochefoucauld

Teaching my sister to read, write, and count gave me, from the age of six onwards, a sense of pride in my own efficacy...I felt I was at last creating something real.

Simone de Beauvior

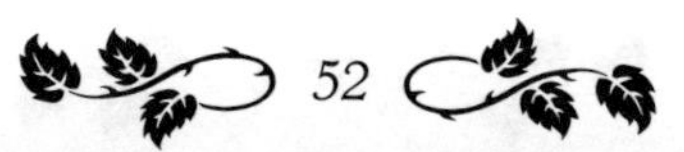

What is a sister?
She is your teacher,
your defense attorney,
even your shrink.

Barbara Alpert

Family is the we of me.

Carson McCullers

Call it a clan, call it a network,
call it a tribe, call it a family.
Whatever you call it, whoever you are,
you need it.

Jane Howard

From birth to death, the sibling
relationship undergoes an amazing
amount of change and development all
because the players involved
continue to evolve and grow.

Susan Scarf Merrell

Sibling relationships are often life's
longest-lasting relationships.

Stephen P. Banks

Sister is probably the most competitive relationship within the family, but once sisters are grown, it becomes the strongest relationship.

Margaret Mead

She rides in the front seat:
She's my older sister.

Carly Simon

When there's a sibling,
there's a quibbling.

Selma Raskin

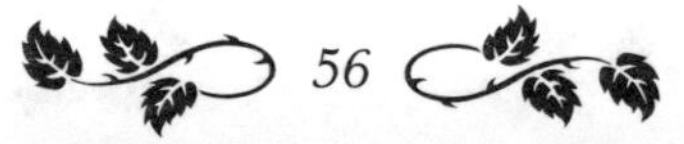

You can't give up a sister. You were born with her and you die with her.

Elizabeth Mead Steig

Family faces are magic mirrors. Looking at people who belong to us, we see past, present, and future.

Gail Lumet Buckley

Brothers and sisters are as close as hands and feet.

Vietnamese Proverb

It takes a heap of livin' in a house
to make it home.

Edgar Guest

When you look at your life,
the greatest happiness is
family happiness.

Dr. Joyce Brothers

Home ought to be our clearinghouse,
the place from which we go forth...
ready for life.

Kathleen Norris

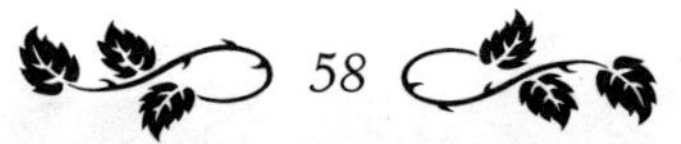

What can we do
to promote world peace?
Go home and
love your family.

Mother Teresa
Upon receiving the Nobel Prize

Sisterhood is a sibling revelry.

Karen Brown

The need for family — for nurture, stability, sharing — does not stay behind when one leaves one's home.

Karen Lindsey

Home is where you learn values. It's the responsibility of the family.

Melba Moore

The family is that dear octopus from whose tentacles we never quite escape, nor, in our innermost hearts, ever quite wish to.

Dodie Smith

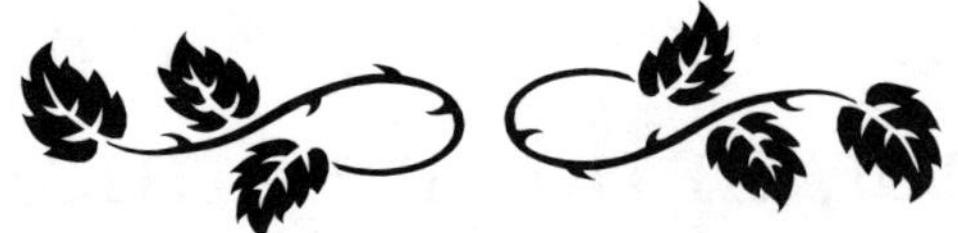

5

A Best Friend

Eventually, it happens: sisters become the dearest of friends. Certainly there are exceptions: sisters who for various reasons lose their connections with each other. Most sisters, however, enjoy a fruitful friendship that ripens with age.

Sisters who are wise enough and lucky enough to craft a lifelong friendship are blessed, as the following quotations clearly attest.

To have a loving relationship with a sister is not simply to have a buddy or a confidante — it is to have a soulmate for life.

Victoria Secunda

The sister relationship parallels friendship, but additional dynamics are at work.

Dee Brestin

The bond between sisters is unique, stretching and bending through periods of closeness and distance, but almost never breaking.

Carol Saline

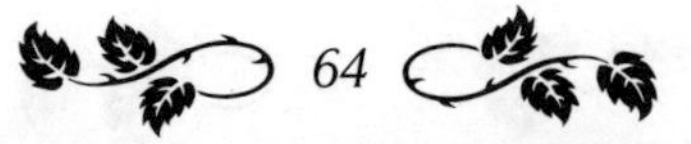

Sooner or later, sisters turn into best friends.

Angela Beasley Freeman

It is better to make one's friendships at home.

Plutarch

A friend you might have to give up. You can't give up a sister. You were born with her and you die with her.

Elizabeth Mead Steig

Over the years, sisters generally draw closer, knitting together their defenses out of common threads.

Elizabeth Fishel

Now that I am an adult, my siblings have become even more important: we age together.

Jane Mersky Leder

We were friends throughout life with that intimacy but also — as children — with that squabbling.

Alva Myrdal

The tie of a sister is near and dear indeed.

Charlotte Brontë

My sister is the friend who shows me what I want from other friends.

Michele D' Ambrosio

The best thing about having a sister was that I always had a friend.

Cali Rae Turner

For better or worse, sisters remain sisters, until death do they part.

Brigid McConville

Having a sister is like having a best friend that you can't get rid of. You know whatever you do, they'll still be there.

Amy Li

To throw away an honest friend is,
as it were, to throw your life away.

Sophocles

Even after death, the language
of sisters endures.

Elizabeth Fishel

A friend is a second self.

Cicero

Best friend, my wellspring in the wilderness.

George Eliot

My sister's presence makes the room feel warm and alive.

Anne Morrow Lindbergh

Friends may come and friends may go, but a sister remains forever.

Arlene F. Benedict

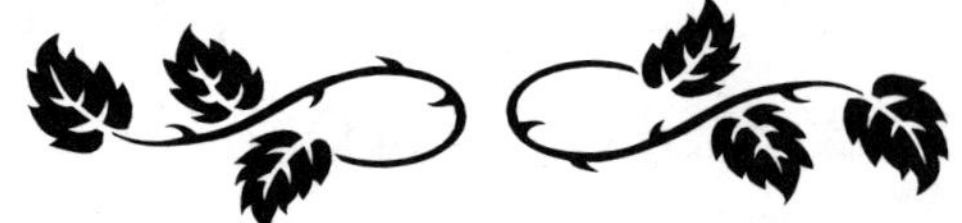

6

Support

In times of hardship or heartbreak, sisters help sisters. A caring, loving sister — biological or otherwise — is a powerful source of emotional strength in good times and bad.

The following words of wisdom remind us that sisterly support provides a firm foundation for the rigors of life.

While friends may come and go, sisters are a permanent part of the personal landscape. Perhaps that's why sisterly alliances are strengthened during times of hardship. Simply put, sisters stick together.

Angela Beasley Freeman

Dear sister, you can't think how I depend on you, and when you're not there the color goes out of my life.

Virginia Woolf

We four sisters were there for each other in good times and bad, for richer and poorer, in sickness and in health… till death do we part.

Dianne Lennon

Your sister believes you are wise, especially when you come to her for advice.

Karen Brown

No matter how infrequently sisters may see each other, when the chips are really down, the sisters' bond comes into its own once again.

Brigid McConville

Blessed is the influence of one true, loving human soul upon another.

George Eliot

Sweet is the voice of a sister in the season of sorrow, and wise is the counsel of those who love us.

Benjamin Disraeli

It's not the load that breaks you down;
it's the way you carry it.

Lena Horne

My sisters can always say or do just the
right things to make me feel better.

Barbara Mandrell

Women whose eyes have been washed clear
with tears get broad vision, and that makes
them little sisters to all the world.

Dorothy Dix

Surround yourself with people who lift you higher.

Oprah Winfrey

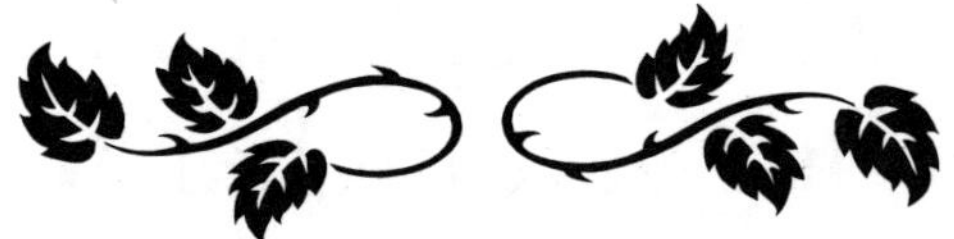

7

History

Childhood memories are the mutual possession of the sisters who helped create them. Sisters are forever linked by a common history; that's why sisters understand sisters.

Memories create the colorful tapestry of experiences that give life its richness and meaning. Savvy sisters treasure their experiences; they remember the good times with fondness, and they share their memories with each other.

Our brothers and sisters are there for us from the dawn of our personal stories to the inevitable dusk.

Susan Scarf Merrell

Memory is a painter.
It paints pictures of the past.

Grandma Moses

Childhood memories live
beneath the surface
of a sister's mind,
never quite forgotten....

Brigid McConville

There is no one else on earth
with whom you share so much
personal history.

Judith Viorst

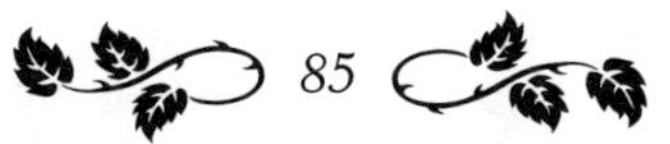

It suddenly became clear to me that my sister was the one person who had known me for the longest time.

Elizabeth Jolley

What sets sisters apart
from brothers — and also from friends —
is a very intimate meshing of the heart,
the soul, and the mystical cords
of memory.

Carol Saline

What greater thing
is there for human
souls than to feel that
they are joined for life —
to be with each other
in silent, unspeakable
memories.

George Eliot

Our siblings are the only people
who can truly share all of our happy
and unhappy childhood memories with us.

Susan Scarf Merrell

There are so many memories...
the interweaving of those funny, joyful,
angry, painful and historic memories creates
the foundation on which every
sister-relationship rests.

Carol Saline

No one knows better than a sister how we grew up and who were our favorite friends, teachers and toys.

Dale V. Atkins

Often in old age, sisters become each other's chosen companions. In addition to shared memories of childhood ... they share memories of the same home, the same homemaking style, and the small prejudices about housekeeping that carry the echoes of their mother's voice.

Margaret Mead

Sisters share a mutual knowledge of the intuitive and unspoken.

Brigid McConville

Her sister's parallel life is a "yardstick," or "touchstone" — a constant point of reference from which she can gauge her own identity.

Brigid McConville

Our siblings push buttons that can cast us back into the roles we felt sure we'd let go of long ago — the baby, the peacekeeper, the caretaker.... It doesn't seem to matter how much time has elapsed or how far we've traveled.

Jane Mersky Leder

Friends can be close, but none so close as one who shares your history, lineage, legacy.

Alda Ellis

God gave us memories so that we might have roses in December.

James M. Barrie

As siblings we were inextricably bound.... No matter how old we got or how often we tried to show another face, reality was filtered through yesterday's memories.

Jane Mersky Leder

May I forget what ought to be forgotten and recall unfailingly all that ought to be recalled.

Laura Palmer

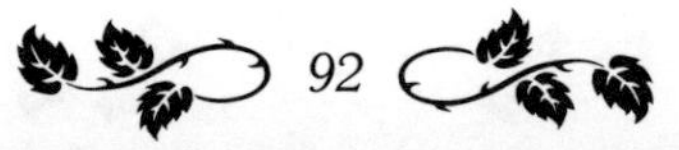

Some memories are better than anything that can ever happen to one again.

Willa Cather

To be able to enjoy one's past is to be able to live twice.

Martial

One's sister is a part of one's essential self, an eternal presence of one's heart and soul and memory.

Susan Cahill

We wove a web in childhood,
A web of sunny air.

Charlotte Brontë

Blessed be childhood, which brings down something of heaven into the midst of our rough earthliness.

Henri Frédéric Amiel

The events of childhood do not pass, but repeat themselves like seasons of the year.

Eleanor Farjeon

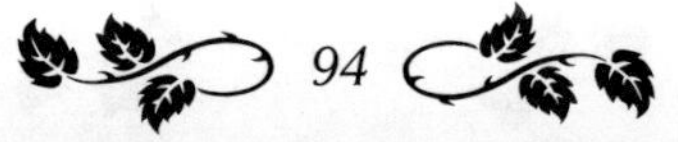

Bliss in possessions
will not last;
remembered joys
are never past.

James Montgomery

What we remember from childhood we remember forever — permanent ghosts, stamped, imprinted, eternally seen.

Cynthia Ozick

It is in coming to terms with the sense of being the same and different which is at the heart of the sister's relationship.

Brigid McConville

The pull between sisters is the realization of similarity versus the need for difference.

Elizabeth Fishel

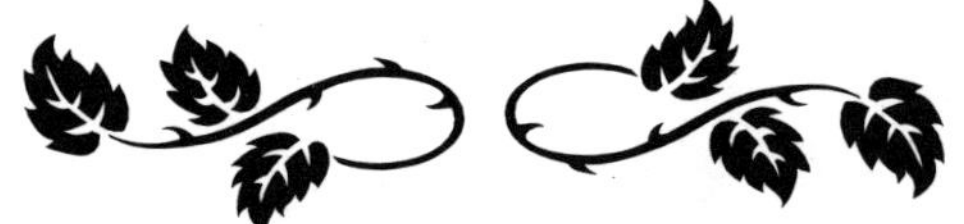

8

Forever

Sisterhood is a bond that stretches throughout life and beyond. Loving sisters encourage each other, they support each other, they counsel and heal each other, and in doing so, each sister leaves her indelible mark upon the other and therefore upon eternity.

As grateful siblings can attest, sisters are forever. Thank goodness!

Remember you are always in the heart — tucked so close there is no chance of escape — of your sister.

Katherine Mansfield

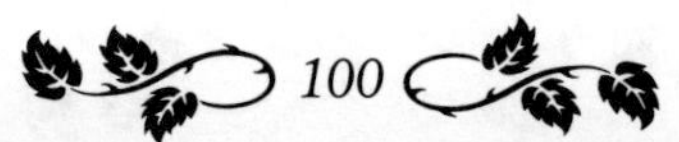

We are sisters.
We will always be sisters.

Nancy Kelton

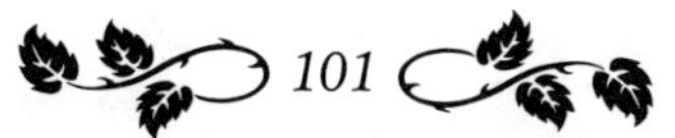

How lucky we are
to have a sister with us
on the journey of life.

Arlene F. Benedict

I recognize how crucial my relationship with my sisters is in the definition of my self.

Barbara Mathias

If Sadie is molasses, then I'm vinegar. Sadie is sugar and I'm spice... but we were best friends from Day One.

Bessie Delany

Every woman
is like — yet unlike —
her sister.

Brigid McConville

Knowing a sister is like having a sixth-sense perception of someone.

Brigid McConville

Sisters — As youngsters they may share popsicles, chewing gum, hair dryers and bedrooms. When they grow up, they share confidences, careers, children, and chats.

Roxanne Brown

My sisters taught me how to live.

Georgette Wasserstein

Sisters, whatever their stories,
instinctively know how
fortunate they are.

Susan Ripps

Let us make one point…
that we meet each other with a smile….
Smile at each other and make time for
each other in your family.

Mother Teresa

From birth to death, sisters model and pattern their scripts after each other. They take cues from each other about the way life is or might be.

Elizabeth Fishel

Many women say their lives have evolved as a pattern interwoven with their sisters'. A sister's influence may make itself felt at all levels.

Brigid McConville

There is more life where my sister is.

Anne Morrow Lindbergh

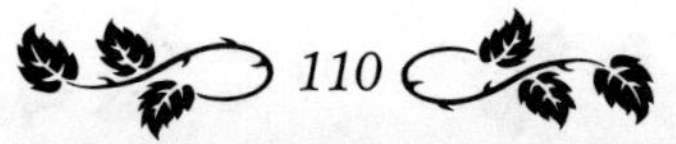

After so long together,
my sister and I are,
in some ways,
like one person.

Sadie Delany

Your sister is
your other self.
She is your alter ego,
your reflection,
your foil,
your shadow.

Barbara Mathias

Now that I am without your company, I feel not only that I am deprived of a very dear sister, but that I have lost half of myself.

Beatrice D' Este

What is a sister?
She is your mirror,
shining back at you
with a world
of possibilities.

Barbara Alpert

A sister is both your mirror —
and your opposite.

Elizabeth Fishel

Although as an adult, you and your sister
may live in very different worlds,
you share the source from which
you learned about life.

Dale V. Atkins

Having a sister means having
one of the most beautiful and unique
of human relationships.

Robert Strand

Sisters define their rivalry in terms of competition for the golden cup of parental love.

Elizabeth Fishel

It occurs to me that one can never fully grow up with one's sister. In some secret place, we always remain seven and eight.

Patricia Foster

Each family of sisters has a language
and a turn of phrase all its own.

Barbara Mathias

When my sister and I talked together,
the words had meaning yet did not weigh
too heavily upon us.

Simone de Beauvoir

With a sister, you learn to love and to argue, to share and to spat.

Dale V. Atkins

More than Santa Claus,
your sister knows
when you've been
bad and good.

Linda Sunshine

One of the greatest things in life is being able to play the role of a helping sister.

Barbara Mandrell

Sometimes, the light at
the end of the tunnel
is your sister
with a flashlight.

Karen Brown

If you have a sister still living, hug her!

Patti LaBelle

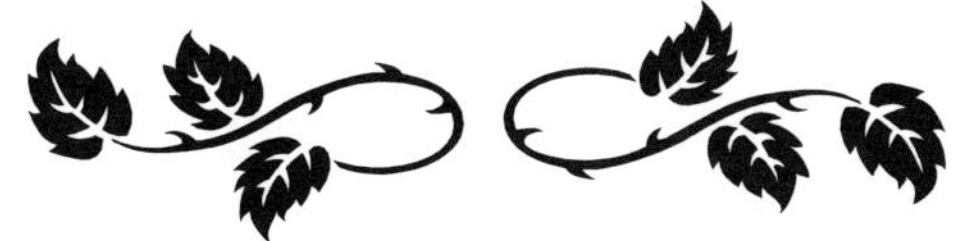

About the Author

Mary Carlisle Beasley is a writer who lives and works in Nashville, Tennessee and is the author of numerous books including several published by DELANEY STREET PRESS.

About DELANEY STREET PRESS

DELANEY STREET PRESS publishes a series of books designed to inspire and entertain readers of all ages. DELANEY STREET books are distributed by Walnut Grove Press. For more information, call 1-800-256-8584.

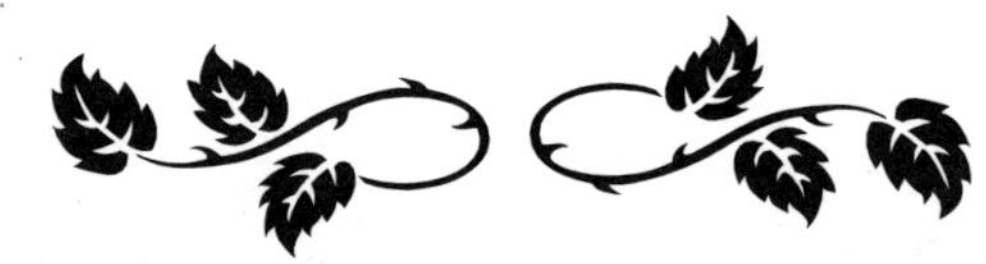